FAV(
TO TI

Arranged for Private Prayer

•

With a Short Helpful Meditation
Before Each Novena

By

REV. LAWRENCE G. LOVASIK, S.V.D.
Divine Word Missionary

Illustrated in Color

CATHOLIC BOOK PUBLISHING CO.
New Jersey

NIHIL OBSTAT: Francis J. McAree, S.T.D.
Censor Librorum

IMPRIMATUR: ✠ Patrick J. Sheridan, D.D.
Vicar General, Archdiocese of New York

The Nihil Obstat and Imprimatur are official declarations that a book or pamphlet is free of doctrinal or moral error. No implication is contained therein that those who have granted the Nihil Obstat and Imprimatur agree with the contents, opinions or statements expressed.

ABBREVIATIONS OF THE BOOKS OF THE BIBLE

Acts—Acts of the Apostles	Jb—Job	Nm—Numbers
Am—Amos	Jdt—Judith	Ob—Obadiah
Bar—Baruch	Jer—Jeremiah	Phil—Philippians
1 Chr—1 Chronicles	Jgs—Judges	Phlm—Philemon
2 Chr—2 Chronicles	Jl—Joel	Prv—Proverbs
Col—Colossians	Jn—John	Ps(s)—Psalms
1 Cor—1 Corinthians	1 Jn—1 John	1 Pt—1 Peter
2 Cor—2 Corinthians	2 Jn—2 John	2 Pt—2 Peter
Dn—Daniel	3 Jn—3 John	Rom—Romans
Dt—Deuteronomy	Jon—Jonah	Ru—Ruth
Eccl—Ecclesiastes	Jos—Joshua	Rv—Revelation
Eph—Ephesians	Jude—Jude	Sir—Sirach
Est—Esther	1 Kgs—1 Kings	1 Sm—1 Samuel
Ex—Exodus	2 Kgs—2 Kings	2 Sm—2 Samuel
Ez—Ezekiel	Lam—Lamentations	Song—Song of Songs
Ezr—Ezra	Lk—Luke	Tb—Tobit
Gal—Galatians	Lv—Leviticus	1 Thes—1 Thessalonians
Gn—Genesis	Mal—Malachi	2 Thes—2 Thessalonians
Hb—Habakkuk	1 Mc—1 Maccabees	Ti—Titus
Heb—Hebrews	2 Mc—2 Maccabees	1 Tm—1 Timothy
Hg—Haggai	Mi—Micah	2 Tm—2 Timothy
Hos—Hosea	Mk—Mark	Wis—Wisdom
Is—Isaiah	Mt—Matthew	Zec—Zechariah
Jas—James	Na—Nahum	Zep—Zephaniah
	Neh—Nehemiah	

(T-36)

FOREWORD

A NOVENA means nine days of public or private prayer for some special occasion or intention. Its origin goes back to the nine days that the disciples and Mary spent together in prayer between the Ascension and Pentecost Sunday. Over the centuries many Novenas have been highly indulgenced by the Church.

To make a Novena means to persevere in prayer asking for some favor over a period of nine days in succession or nine weeks. It means fulfilling our Lord's teaching that we must continue praying and never lose confidence. This confidence is based on our Lord's words: "Ask, and you shall receive; seek, and you shall find; knock, and it shall be opened to you. For everyone who asks receives; everyone who seeks finds; and to whoever knocks, it shall be opened" (Lk 11: 9-10).

The Holy Spirit is the Third Person of the Trinity. He is "the Person-Love, the Uncreated Gift, Who is the Eternal Source of every gift that comes from God in the order of Creation, the direct Principle and, in a certain sense, the Subject of God's self-communication in the order of Grace" (Pope John Paul II).

It is the specific work of the Holy Spirit to form the Christian to be a Christian. When Christ was leaving the world, He told His Apostles that they would not be deprived of a guide. Another would succeed Him to lead them heavenward. That other was the Holy Spirit, Who came at Pentecost and helped the little band of Christ convert the world.

The Holy Spirit is the Love of God personified. That Love has all the gentleness and understanding of maternal affection. It comes naturally, therefore, to the Third Person of the Blessed Trinity to cherish, to encourage, and to give consolation to those of God's children who are falling by the wayside under the burdens of living on earth.

They are wise who have recourse to the Holy Spirit in all the issues of life, temporal as well as spiritual. This recourse to Him should not be occasional or particular; it should be continual and in regard to all necessities. And one way this can be done is by making use of the Novenas and spiritual exercises to the Holy Spirit found in this book.

Try to talk with God during your Novena. Absolute sincerity is most important. And as you grow in daily reflection and prayer, you will find yourself talking to God with much the same ease as you would converse with a close friend.

Use your own words in this simple, intimate chat with God, and such chats will gradually become your own personal, individual way of prayer. You will find that the Holy Spirit is enlightening your mind and strengthening your will to do God's Will.

Father Lawrence G. Lovasik, S.V.D.

CONTENTS

NOVENA FOR THE HELP OF THE HOLY SPIRIT

MEDITATION

THE Holy Spirit is God, and Third Person of the Holy Trinity, really God, the same as the Father and the Son are really God. He is the love of the Father and the Son.

Christ promised that this Spirit of Truth would come and would remain within us. "I will ask the Father and He will give you another Advocate—to dwell with you always: the Spirit of truth, Whom the world cannot accept, since it neither sees Him nor knows Him; but you will know Him because He dwells with you and will be in you" (Jn 14:16-17).

The Holy Spirit came at Pentecost, never to depart. Fifty days after Easter, on Pentecost Sunday, He changed the Apostles from weak fearful men to brave men of faith that Christ needed to spread His Gospel to the nations.

The Holy Spirit is present in a special way in the Church, the community of those who believe in Christ as Lord. He helps the Church to continue the work of Christ in the world. By His presence people are moved by His grace to unite themselves with God and human beings in sincere love and to fulfill their duties to God and neighbor. He makes the Church pleasing to God because of the Divine life of grace that He gives. By the power of the Gospel He makes the Church grow. He renews her with His Gifts, and leads her to perfect union with Jesus.

The Holy Spirit guides the Pope, bishops, and priests of the Church in their work of teaching Christ's doctrine, guiding souls, and giving God's grace to the people through the Sacraments. He directs all the work of Christ in the Church—the care of the sick, the teaching of children, the guidance of youth, the comforting of the sorrowful, the support of the needy.

We should honor the Holy Spirit by loving Him as our God and by letting Him guide us in life. St. Paul reminds us to do so. "Do you not know that you are the temple of God, and that the Spirit of God dwells in you?" (1 Cor 3:16).

Since the Holy Spirit is always with us if we are in the state of grace, we should often ask Him for the light and strength we need to live a holy life and to save our soul. (The universal symbol of the Holy Spirit is a *dove*.)

THE WORD OF GOD

"Amen, amen, I say to you, no one can enter into the Kingdom of God unless he is born of water and the Spirit. Flesh begets flesh, Spirit begets spirit." —Jn 3:5-6

"These things I have told you while I was still with you. The Advocate, the Holy Spirit Whom the Father will send in My Name, will instruct you in everything and bring to your mind all that I told you." —Jn 14:25-26

"When the days of Pentecost were drawing to a close, they were all together in one place. Suddenly, there came a sound from heaven as of a strong, driving wind, and it filled the whole house where they were sitting. They saw what seemed to be tongues of fire that separated and settled upon each of them. They were all filled with the Holy Spirit and began to speak in foreign tongues as the Spirit enabled them to do." —Acts 2:1-4

"To each person the manifestation of the Spirit is given for the common good. To one through the Spirit is given the message of wisdom, to another the message of knowledge by means of the same Spirit, to another faith by the same Spirit, to another gifts of healing by that same Spirit, to another the working of miracles, to another prophecy, to another the discernment of spirits, to another speaking in tongues, and to still another the interpretation of tongues. But all these are the work of one and the same Spirit, Who allots to everyone according as He wills." —1 Cor 12:7-11

NOVENA PRAYERS
Novena Prayer

HOLY Spirit, Third Person of the Blessed Trinity, Spirit of truth, love, and holiness, proceeding from the Father and the Son, and equal to Them in all things, I adore You and love You with all my heart.

Dearest Holy Spirit, confiding in Your deep, personal love for me, I am making this Novena for the following request, if it should be Your holy Will to grant it:*(Mention your request).*

Teach me, Divine Spirit, to know and seek my last end; grant me the holy fear of God; grant me true contrition and patience. Do not let me fall into sin. Give me an increase of faith, hope, and charity, and bring forth in my soul all the virtues proper to my state of life.

Make me a faithful disciple of Jesus and an obedient child of the Church. Give me efficacious grace sufficient to keep the Commandments and to receive the Sacraments worthily. Give me the four Cardinal Virtues, Your Seven Gifts, Your Twelve Fruits. Raise me to perfection in the state of life to which You have called me and lead me through a happy death to everlasting life. I ask this through Christ our Lord. Amen.

Consecration

HOLY Spirit, Divine Spirit of light and love, I consecrate to You my understanding, heart, and will, my whole being, for time and for eternity. May my understanding be always submissive to Your heavenly inspirations and to the teaching of the Catholic Church, of which You are the infallible Guide. May my heart be ever inflamed with the love of God and of my neighbor. May my will be ever conformed to the Divine Will. May my whole life be faithful to the imitation of the life and virtues of our Lord and Savior Jesus Christ, to Whom with the Father and You be honor and glory forever.

God, Holy Spirit, Infinite Love of the Father and the Son, through the pure hands of Mary, Your Immaculate Spouse, I place myself this day, and all the days of my life, upon Your chosen altar, the Divine Heart of Jesus, as a sacrifice to You, consuming fire, being firmly resolved now more than ever to hear Your voice and to do in all things Your most holy and adorable Will. Amen.

Prayer

GRANT, we beg of You, Almighty God, that we may so please Your Holy Spirit by our earnest prayers, that we may, by His grace, be freed from all temptations and merit to receive the forgiveness of our sins. Through Christ our Lord. Amen.

Come, Holy Spirit, Creator Blest!

COME, Holy Spirit, Creator blest!
And in our souls take up Your rest;
Come, with Your grace and heavenly aid,
To fill the hearts that You have made.

O Comforter, to You do we cry,
O heavenly Gift of God Most High;
O Fount of life and Fire of love,
And sweet Anointing from above!

You in Your sevenfold Gifts are known;
You, Finger of God's hand, we own;
You, Promise of the Father, You,
Who do the tongue with power imbue.

Kindle our senses from above
And make our hearts o'erflow with love;
With patience firm and virtue high,
The weakness of our flesh supply.

Far from us drive the foe we dread,
And grant us Your true peace instead;
So shall we not, with You for Guide,
Turn from the path of life aside.

Oh, may Your grace on us bestow
The Father and the Son to know;
And You, through endless times confessed,
Of Both the eternal Spirit blest.

Now to the Father and the Son,
Who rose from death, be glory given,
With You, O holy Comforter,
Henceforth by all in earth and heaven.
Amen.

℣. Send forth Your Spirit and they shall be created;

℟. *And You shall renew the face of the earth.*

LET us pray. God, You have taught the hearts of Your faithful people by sending them the light of Your Holy Spirit. Grant us by the same Spirit to have a right judgment in all things and evermore to rejoice in His holy comfort. Through Christ our Lord. ℟. *Amen.*

NOVENA FOR THE COMING OF THE HOLY SPIRIT

MEDITATION

EVEN though devotion to the Holy Spirit under-
lies all our devotions, if they are devotions ap-
proved by the Church, such implicit devotion does
not satisfy our obligations to the Holy Spirit. There
are many reasons why every Catholic should have
special devotion to the Holy Spirit. We will recall
only three of them here.

First, because He is a Divine Person, coequal
with the Father and the Son, we are bound to adore
Him and honor Him, even as we honor the First and
Second Persons of the Holy Trinity. He inspired
those words of bitter complaint wherein He asks
His people, why they do not honor Him as their God
if they believe in Him (Is 1:2-4).

Secondly, gratitude for the gift of faith should
arouse us to devotion. Pope Leo XIII says in one of
his beautiful instructions to the Christian world: "We
earnestly desire that piety may increase and be inflamed toward the Holy Spirit to Whom especially all
of us owe the grace of following the path of truth."

Lastly, St. Paul tells us: "The charity of God is poured forth into our hearts, by the Holy Spirit, Who is given to us." We need this supernatural charity to save our souls; therefore, we should be devoted to Him Who gives it to us. In fact Jesus Himself gave His Apostles this motive when He told them: "It is expedient for you that I go, for if I go not, the Paraclete [the Holy Spirit] will not come to you."

FIRST DAY

Come, O Holy Spirit, come!
From Your bright and blissful Home
Rays of healing light impart.

O GOD, You taught the hearts of Your faithful by the light of the Holy Spirit. Grant that by the gift of the same Spirit I may be always truly wise and ever rejoice in His consolations. Amen.

SECOND DAY

Come, Father of the poor,
Source of gifts that will endure
Light of ev'ry human heart.

O HOLY Spirit, Father of the poor, come fill my poverty-stricken soul out of the plenty of Your eternal riches. Warn me, I beg You, of every opportunity in my daily round of duty, to lay up treasures where no thief approaches nor moth corrupts, that I may enjoy them together with You forever. Amen.

THIRD DAY

You of all consolers best,
Of the soul most kindly Guest,
Quick'ning courage do bestow.

O DIVINE Consoler, and of all Comforters the best, to You do I come in trouble and distress. May You, in the all-powerful Name of Jesus, our Redeemer, and out of love for Mary, our sorrowful Mother and Your chaste Spouse, come to my assistance and comfort me in all my trials and tribulations. Amen.

FOURTH DAY

In hard labor You are rest,
In the heat You refresh best,
And solace give in our woe.

O GOD, You bestowed the Holy Spirit on the Apostles. Grant to Your people the effect of their pious prayers, that on those to whom You have given grace, You may also bestow peace. Amen.

FIFTH DAY

O most blessed Light Divine,
Let Your radiance in us shine,
And our inmost being fill.

MAY the Paraclete, Who proceeds from You, enlighten my mind, I beseech You, O Lord; and even as Your Son has promised, may He lead me into all truth. Amen.

SIXTH DAY

Nothing good by man is thought,
Nothing right by him is wrought,
When he spurns Your gracious Will.

SEND down, I beseech You, O Lord, the Holy Spirit in His might, to the merciful purifying of my heart and to my sure deliverance from all danger. Amen.

SEVENTH DAY

Cleanse our souls from sinful stain,
Lave our dryness with Your rain,
Heal our wounds and mend our way.

BURN up, O Lord, my reins and heart in the fire of the Holy Spirit; that chaste of body and clean of heart, my service may be well pleasing to You. Amen.

EIGHTH DAY

Bend the stubborn heart and will,
Melt the frozen, warm the chill,
Guide the steps that go astray.

HOLY Spirit, Spirit of Truth, come into my heart. Give to all peoples the brightness of Your light, that they may be well pleasing to You in unity of faith. Amen.

NINTH DAY

On the faithful who in You,
Trust with childlike piety,
Deign Your sevenfold gift to send.
Give them virtue's rich increase,
Saving grace to die in peace,
Give them joys that never end. Amen. Alleluia.

SEND down upon me, I beseech You, O Lord, the Holy Spirit, that, inspired and encouraged by Him, I may comply with the duties of my state, carry my crosses patiently, and grow daily in Christian perfection. Grant me, through the same Divine Spirit, the intentions of this Novena or what is most conducive to my eternal salvation and Your glory. Amen.

NOVENA FOR THE GIFTS
OF THE HOLY SPIRIT

MEDITATION

THE Holy Spirit lives in us. He makes us holy by imparting to us *sanctifying grace,* God's own life in us, and by giving us the *supernatural virtues* of faith, hope, and love that come with it. The Holy Spirit also gives us *actual grace,* the help we need for mind and will in order to lead good lives. It is a special help that imparts light to our mind and strength to our will in order to do good.

The Holy Spirit helps us do good in various ways. Most of all, He does it by endowing us with His *seven Gifts, twelve Fruits, and various Charisma.*

The traditional names of the Gifts of the Holy Spirit are: Wisdom, Understanding, Counsel, Fortitude, Knowledge, Piety, and Fear of the Lord. They are, in reality, supernatural graces for a more perfect Christian life.

To live a human life we need a human organism, consisting of body, senses, vital spirit, intelligence, will, memory, and the like. To live a Christian life, that is, a Divine life, which Christ has brought from heaven, we need a kind of supernatural, Divine organism. This is constituted by sanctifying grace that sanctifies or divinizes the soul in its being by the three theological virtues (faith, hope, and love) and the four cardinal virtues (knowledge, justice, fortitude, and temperance).

Transformed, revived, and divinized by this supernatural organism, Christians are already set in motion to begin the Divine life. They are already on the way to know, will, love, and act after the manner of Christ and the Trinity.

The Gifts of the Spirit help us to be more conformed to Christ, make us more docile to His suggestions, more submissive to His inspirations, and more pliable to His directions. If we remain open to these Gifts and cooperate with them, we will become ever more the persons God wants us to be—other Christs.

Three of the Gifts (Fear, Piety, and Fortitude) perfect the will. The other four (Wisdom, Understanding, Counsel, and Knowledge) perfect the intellect. They are united by love, by which the Holy Spirit dwells in us.

FIRST DAY—IMPORTANCE OF THE GIFTS

The Word of God

"The Spirit of the Lord shall rest upon Him: the Spirit of Wisdom and Understanding, the Spirit of Counsel and Fortitude, the Spirit of Knowledge and Piety. And He shall be filled with the Spirit of the Fear of the Lord."

—Is 11:2-3

Consideration

WE shall strive during this Novena to obtain an increase of the seven Gifts of the Holy Spirit, over and above the special favors we shall ask from the Divine Spirit. The Gifts of the Holy Spirit are permanent supernatural dispositions given to us with grace, to make the soul attentive and responsive to the movements of the Third Person of the Adorable Trinity. Very appropriately have they been compared to the sails of a ship, which, when spread, carry the craft swiftly and smoothly over its course.

When the inspirations of the Holy Spirit find the Gifts spread like sails in the soul, they waft safely over the sea of life to the haven of eternal happiness. Those Christians who through indolence allow the gifts to lie dormant, are like ships dismantled, whose sails lie in the bottom of the boat, useless. Who has not felt many a time, even immediately after coming from the sacred tribunal of Penance, the necessity of some such impelling power? Therefore, let us beseech the Holy Spirit for an increase of these necessary Gifts.

Prayer

ALMIGHTY and eternal God, You have regenerated us by water and the Holy Spirit, and have given us forgiveness of all sins. Be pleased to send forth from heaven upon us Your sevenfold Spirit, the Spirit of Wisdom and Understanding, the Spirit of Counsel and Fortitude, the Spirit of Knowledge and of Piety, and fill us with the Spirit of Holy Fear. Amen.

To obtain the special favors and blessings for which you are making this Novena and also an increase of the seven Gifts of the Holy Spirit recite 7 times the Glory be to the Father.

SECOND DAY—THE GIFT OF HOLY FEAR

The Word of God

"The Fear of the Lord is the beginning of wisdom."
—Wis 1:12

Consideration

THE irreligious man often fears that there may possibly be a God and a time of retribution. O what a base fear; a fear that he tries to bury in oblivion by leading a riotous, sinful life. With such fear we are not concerned. The Gift of Holy Fear fills us with a sovereign respect for God, and makes us dread above all things to offend Him. It is fear like that of a dutiful son, who will shun certain company of whom he knows no evil, but with whom his parents do not wish him to associate. He simply respects his parents' wishes.

It is a fear that arises from reverence and submission toward those we love and esteem. It measures the malice of sin, not by the world's standards, but by those of heaven. If it does not suggest very noble deeds in God's service, at least it keeps us from going over to the enemy's camp. For this reason we, poor sin-

ners, need the Gift of Holy Fear. Let us therefore pray fervently for it.

Prayer

COME, O blessed Spirit of Holy Fear, penetrate my inmost heart, that I may set You,
my Lord and God, before my face for ever; and
shun all things that can offend You, so that I
may be made worthy to appear before the pure
eyes of Your Divine Majesty in the heaven of
heavens, where You live and reign in the unity
of the ever Blessed Trinity, God forever and
ever.

Glory be to the Father, etc. (7 times.)

THIRD DAY—THE GIFT OF PIETY

The Word of God

"Piety is profitable in all respects for it has the promise of
the present life as well as that which is to come." —1 Tm
4:8

Consideration

THE Gift of Piety is the Gift through which
the Holy Spirit calls to the service of God
and man, the mistress of virtues, charity. It
prompts us to love God not because of His
majesty, but because He is our Father. It makes
us love whatever is near and dear to our Divine
Savior, beginning with His Immaculate Mother
and going down the scale to the most aban-
doned on earth and in purgatory.

The Gift of Piety, which bids us love our
Father in heaven, stirs up our affections for our

father and mother in the flesh, our own dear parents, for our fathers in God, the Pope, Bishops, and Priests, for our home, our Church, and our country. Pride and envy beget chauvinism, which is false patriotism and narrowmindedness; the Gift of Piety begets real patriotism. Let us, therefore, pray fervently for this beautiful Gift.

Prayer

COME, O blessed Spirit of Piety, possess my heart, incline it to a true faith in You, to a holy love of You, my God, and of all my fellow creatures for Your sake. Amen.

Glory be to the Father, etc. (7 times.)

FOURTH DAY—THE GIFT OF KNOWLEDGE

The Word of God

"Let your heart apply itself to instruction and your ears to words of Knowledge." —Prv 23:12

Consideration

KNOWLEDGE, as a Gift of the Holy Spirit, directs the soul to judge of things, both human and Divine, according to supernatural common sense and not according to the standards of the worldly-wise. Even with supernatural faith in our soul to elevate our reason, how often we detect ourselves talking of temporal gain and loss, success and failure, suffering and pleasure, purely and simply, according to the principles of the worldly-minded!

We fail to pierce the veil of the natural and see in suffering a blessing from God. We have come to think it folly to season our pleasures with a pinch of pepper and salt of mortifications; for example: to determine that we will not remain out later than a certain reasonable hour, when we go out for an evening of innocent pleasure.

In this age of doubt, materialism, pleasure-seeking, what shall we say of the necessity of this Gift to enable us to distinguish good from evil, innocent pleasure from tainted joy, truth from falsehood, the real good from the apparent good among all the things around us? Let us, therefore, pray earnestly for this Gift.

Prayer

COME, O blessed Spirit of Knowledge, and grant that I may perceive the Will of the Father. Show me the nothingness of earthly things, that I may realize their vanity and use them only for Your glory and my own salvation, looking ever beyond them to You and Your eternal rewards. Amen.

Glory be to the Father, etc. (7 times.)

FIFTH DAY—THE GIFT OF FORTITUDE

The Word of God

"Stephen, full of grace and Fortitude, was working great signs and wonders among the people."   —Acts 6:8

Consideration

FORTITUDE is a Gift of the Holy Spirit strengthening the soul against all natural fear and supporting it to the end in the performance of duty. Daily the soul, in the state of grace, must go forth to fight the good fight of Christ; to do its duty, which, because it is duty, will always be difficult.

The virtue of Fortitude leads us into the battle, but we need special encouragement from the Spirit of God, to enable us to persevere in good, in spite of unforeseen difficulties, hardships, and the grind of routine. That encouragement the Holy Spirit imparts to us through the Gift of Fortitude. Moreover, while we are not called upon to face the roaring lion in the Roman arena like the first Christians, we are bound every day of our lives to fight the roaring lion within us, to struggle against our besetting temptation. God has armed us with the Gift of Fortitude for that purpose.

Let us, therefore, pray for that Gift to enable us to fight perseveringly the good fight of Jesus Christ until it please our Divine Leader to call us from the battlefield of life to enjoy the eternal reward of heaven.

Prayer

COME, O blessed Spirit of Fortitude, uphold my soul in time of trouble and adversity. Sustain my efforts after holiness, strengthen my weakness, give me courage against all the assaults of my enemies. May I never be overcome and separated from You, my God and greatest Good. Amen.

Glory be to the Father, etc. (7 times.)

SIXTH DAY—THE GIFT OF COUNSEL

The Word of God

"Counsel will watch over you, and understanding will guard you."   —Prv 2:11

Consideration

THE Gift of Counsel is a disposition in the soul through which the Holy Spirit prompts us to choose to do the better of two good actions. It is the elder sister of supernatural prudence. Prudence teaches us the A, B, C of Christian life; the Gift of Counsel trains us in the fine arts of Christian perfection.

As this Gift gains greater influence over our actions, the soul begins to realize more and more the full meaning of the words of St. Paul: "All things are lawful to me, but all things are not expedient" (1 Cor 6, 12). This Gift can never be developed in the Christian soul that stops short only of mortal sin in its use and abuse of liberty. Such a rule of conduct will not keep us long from mortal sin, and when mortal sin enters the soul, grace and all the supernatural gifts depart.

Because my use of the things of this world may give my neighbor a pretext for abusing them, it is often expedient for me to hearken to the Counsel of my Divine Guide and refrain from licit pleasures and actions. Above all, as Catholics, we should be as shining lights to our neighbors, going before them in the path of virtue. To do so, we need the gift of Counsel; therefore, let us pray for it.

Prayer

COME, O Spirit of Counsel, help and guide me in all my ways, that I may always do Your holy Will. Incline my heart to that which is good; turn it away from all that is evil, and direct me by the straight path of Your Commandments to that goal of eternal life for which I long. Amen.

Glory be to the Father, etc. (7 times.)

SEVENTH DAY—THE GIFT OF UNDERSTANDING

The Word of God

"Forget not My Law, and let your heart keep My Commandments. . . . And you shall find grace and Understanding."   —Prv 3:1-4

CONSIDERATION

UNDERSTANDING, as a Gift of the Holy Spirit, helps the Christian, in the state of grace, to grasp according to his mental capacity, the meaning of the truths of our holy religion. Perhaps, to many of us, the articles of the Creed are but dry disconnected truths. God gives us the Gift of Understanding to enable us to penetrate the truths of our holy religion in a manner that will enable us to live them.

Many Catholics find the Catholic newspapers flat and unsavory. On Sundays they would like to hear the priest speak of the topics of the times rather than give catechetical instructions. That is because they are imbued with the spirit of the age. They have never become accustomed to thinking seriously of religious subjects. They have no religious, no Catholic, no supernatural ideals.

Perhaps one of the reasons why we do not duplicate the majestic cathedrals of Europe is, because we do not live the religious Mysteries and ideals that inspired those monuments of faith. We need an increase of the Gift of Understanding to make our religion something real and living. Therefore, let us pray fervently for that intention.

Prayer

COME, O Spirit of Understanding, and enlighten my mind, that I may know and believe all the Mysteries of salvation; and may merit at last to see the eternal light in Your Light; and in the light of glory to have a clear vision of You and the Father and the Son. Amen.

Glory be to the Father, etc. (7 times.)

EIGHTH DAY—THE GIFT OF WISDOM

The Word of God

"I called upon God, and the Spirit of Wisdom came upon me." —Wis 7:7

Consideration

WISDOM is that Gift of the Holy Spirit whereby the Divine Spirit raises up our intellect and our heart to rest in God alone. Knowledge tells us the value of earthly things, and how we can enjoy them licitly without offending God; but Wisdom mounts high above them.

Wisdom is the blossom of all the other Gifts. The latter lead us up, step by step, to the throne of God: Wisdom bids us sit down on His footstool and judge all earthly things from that sublime height. Wisdom gives us courage to trample underfoot wealth, honor, and pleasure, if these things—I will not say, impede our salvation—but even cast so much as a shadow between us and our God.

You may be inclined to think that the Gift of Wisdom is only for Saints. You are right when you say this Gift is only for the Saints, but you are wrong if you think that you are not destined to be a Saint. We must all aspire to sanctity. Why not aim high? God will reward the effort. Let us begin today by trying to make an act of thanksgiving for every little cross that falls on us.

Prayer

COME, O Spirit of Wisdom, and reveal to my soul the Mysteries of heavenly things, their exceeding greatness, power, and beauty. Teach me to love them above and beyond all the passing joys and satisfactions of earth. Show me the way by which I may be able to attain them and possess them forever. Amen.

Glory be to the Father, etc. (7 times.)

NINTH DAY—ZEAL FOR THE GLORY OF GOD AND THE PROPAGATION OF THE FAITH

The Word of God

"Zeal for Your house has consumed me." —Ps 69:10

Consideration

THE first great Novena in honor of the Holy Spirit was crowned with an abundant outpouring of the Divine Spirit upon the Apostles. It enkindled within their bosom a zeal that knew not fear of starvation or death, that defied the sword and the cross, that braved storms at sea and bloody persecutions on land, for the propagation of the Faith of Jesus Christ.

Before we close the Novena, let us beg the Holy Spirit to fill the world with zeal for the triumph of right over might, for the triumph of truth over error, for the triumph of honesty and purity over deceit and sensuality. Let us pray that the Divine Spirit may fill many of our young men and young women with zeal for the propagation of the Faith, with courage to sacrifice the comforts of home and the company of parents to labor in the service of Christ and the Church.

Let us pray that He may pour out an abundance of the apostolic spirit upon our priests, missionaries, nuns. Let us pray that He may draw the hearts of heretics and pagans to the one true fold of Jesus Christ, so that from every quarter of the earth the cry will ascend heavenward: Praised be the holy and adorable Trinity; to It be honor and glory forever and ever. Amen.

Prayer

HOLY, Divine Spirit, by the infinite merits of the Passion and Death of Jesus Christ, deign to pour abroad Your most ardent and omnipotent charity into all hearts, so that there may be one Fold and one Shepherd in the whole world; and that we may all come to sing Your Divine praises in heaven forever. Amen.

Glory be to the Father, etc. (7 times.)

NOVENA FOR THE GRACE OF THE SACRAMENTS

MEDITATION

"THE Sacraments are outward signs instituted by Christ to give grace." Hence, they are viewed as acts of Christ Who personally sanctifies each individual through them. At the same time, the Sacraments are acts of the Church, who is entrusted with continuing Christ's priestly office in the world. She carries forth in the world the purpose of the Incarnation.

The Sacraments make available to people throughout the ages the grace and glory of the saving acts of Christ, which took place once and for all in history. The Sacraments are the principal means through which we receive grace in the power of the Holy Spirit. Hence, they provide excellent opportunities for us to enrich our prayer life—for they are prayers in the best sense of the word.

Every celebration of the Sacraments is a prayer of Christ and a cause of prayer for us. Through them we can extend the Eucharistic worship into all space, time, and matter. We can transform our lives and the whole world.

The Sacraments also enable us to pray by reason of the special *character* that they impart to us. This character flows from the priesthood of Christ, which governs all prayer. It forms part of the Sacraments of Baptism, Confirmation, and Holy Orders and is produced in our souls by God through the Holy Spirit. It means that we belong to God forever and that we are the property of Christ so as to share His fundamental prerogatives.

One of the effects of this character is that we receive a share in Christ's priesthood, through the Church to which He has imparted it. Christ has made the Church a royal priesthood and a holy people of God. She is destined to give the Father all the honor and glory that sin has attempted to take away from Him and to provide full salvation to all people and all things.

Through its special character, Baptism gives us a first share in this priesthood of Christ, called the *priesthood of the faithful.* This "priesthood" enables us first of all to join in the offering of the Eucharist. It also empowers us to receive the Sacraments, offer prayer and thanksgiving, lead holy lives, make use of self-denial, and practice an active charity.

Through its special character, Confirmation gives us a second share in this priesthood of Christ. It bestows on us the ability to carry out the prophetic and evangelical function that the Church is called to exercise.

Through its special character, Holy Orders gives us an even more intense share in this priesthood. It configures priests to Christ the priest (in accord with the various grades: bishops, priests, or deacons) and makes them guides, pastors, and heads of the community of believers. This is called the *ministerial priesthood*.

The *priesthood of the faithful* and the *ministerial priesthood* differ from one another both in essence and in degree. Yet they have the quality in common of empowering us to *pray as Christians*. We are enabled to pray with the Sacraments because we possess the characters that inspire our prayer, facilitate our prayer, and perfect our prayer.

FIRST DAY—PRAYING THE SACRAMENTS

The Word of God

"If anyone thirst, let him come to Me and drink. He who believes in Me, as the Scripture says, 'From within him there shall flow rivers of living water.' He said this of the Spirit that those who believed in Him were to receive."

—Jn 7:37-39

Reflection

EVERY Sacrament is an encounter with Christ, Who pardons, heals, and invests us with His priesthood or with His love. Furthermore, it is an encounter with the Jesus of the Paschal Mystery, the Jesus Who eternally established what is the climax of His life and His right to glory: the event of His Death and Resurrection.

In every Sacrament, we are plunged *spiritually but really* into the very act of Jesus dying to sin and rising to new life. Hence, every Sacrament—not only the Eucharist—is a memorial of the Death and Resurrection of Christ.

Prayer To Encounter Jesus in the Sacraments

O JESUS, when we pray with the Sacraments, You become present to us today. We meet You, become transformed in You, and are conformed to You in the manner proper to each Sacrament.

Let me remember that what is important in the reception of each Sacrament is to get myself ready to receive its effect. Help me to get my faith into it, really thirst for it, listen to it, and enter into it with the best possible dispositions—this is tantamount to praying it. Then let me wait, letting the grace of the Sacrament pervade my life. Amen.

SECOND DAY—SACRAMENTS OF GRACE

The Word of God

"Of His fullness we have all received, grace for grace. For the Law was given through Moses; grace and truth came through Jesus Christ." —Jn 1:16-17

Reflection

THE Sacraments are more than static moments in our earthly existence. They are, so to speak, all of our lives. At the moment of the Sacramental celebration, everything is placed in us as if in a seed, but it must be lived out by us in a lifetime.

Each gives us Sacramental grace, namely the particular aspect that—together with the life of Christ given by each Sacrament—is communicated to us and requires an accounting from us. Each Sacrament likens us to an aspect of the personality of the Redeemer. It makes us adopted children of God, reconciled with God, confirmed in our new life, healed of all evil, united in God's love, and filled with the Holy Spirit.

Prayer for Sacramental Grace

O HOLY Spirit, You are the first Gift of Baptism and Confirmation and also the Gift of every Sacrament received with faith. Teach me that the grace of the Sacrament is not something but Someone. It is You—Who intensify Your presence in me, Your activity, Your light, Your tenderness, and Your prayer.

By cooperating with the Sacramental grace, I will be praying the Sacrament with my whole life. I will also be living as well as I am able.

Through each Sacrament refashion me bit by bit and day by day into the image and likeness of Christ. Make me so configured to Him and transfigured in Him that I can exclaim: "I live now; no longer I but Christ lives in me" (Gal 2:20). Amen.

THIRD DAY—THE SACRAMENT OF BAPTISM

The Word of God

"Unless a man be born again of water and the spirit, he cannot enter into the Kingdom of God." —Jn 3:5

Reflection

*B*APTISM makes us children of God sanctified by the Spirit, unites us with Jesus in His Death and Resurrection, cleanses us from sin (both original and personal), and welcomes us into the community of the Church. It relates us permanently to God in a relationship that can never be erased and joins us to the priestly, prophetic, and kingly works of Christ.

Thus, in Baptism, Christ assimilates us to Himself insofar as He is the Son of the Father, and He gives us the spirit of His sonship. *Our task is to cooperate with the grace of the Sacrament by becoming ever more active children of God in the Son of God.*

Prayer To Be a Child of the Church

*G*OD, Holy Spirit, You are the living soul of God's holy Church, and in You alone, dwelling in the Church as in a living tabernacle, the great Mystery of the Church of Christ and its wonderful manifestations are made possible.

I also have been baptized into the unity of that body of which Christ is the Head. Make me a partaker of all those graces that flow from Jesus upon all the members of His Mystical Body. Let the rays of holiness that You shed on this Church be reflected in my soul.

You Who have spoken through the Prophets of old, and now speak to us in the voice of holy Church, make me an obedient and faithful child of this One, Holy, Catholic, and Apostolic Church, which is ever illumined by Your light, ever guided by Your hand, ever preserved from error by Your indwelling presence.

Built upon this rock of the Church, I shall myself be firm as a rock. Clinging to the chair of Peter, my faith shall not fail. Sailing in the bark of Peter, I have no reason to fear shipwreck and can confidently hope to reach the harbor of a happy eternity.

Blessed Spirit of God, make me appreciate the great, inestimable happiness of being a child of holy Church. O Church of the living God, bride of Christ, home of the Holy Spirit, how dear you are to me! You are the love of Christ's Heart, the reward of His toil, made white in His Blood, nourished by His Flesh! Spirit of Truth, keep me always in the spirit of filial love and submission to holy Church. Amen.

FOURTH DAY—THE SACRAMENT OF CONFIRMATION

The Word of God

"Now it is God . . . Who has anointed us, Who has also stamped us with His seal and has given us the Spirit as a pledge in our hearts." —2 Cor 1:21-22

Reflection

THROUGH the Sacrament of *Confirmation,* the Holy Spirit comes once more to us with new grace and new strength to lead the Christian life. We are empowered to live in the world as witnesses of Christ and as helpers of other human beings.

Thus, in Confirmation, Christ assimilates us to Himself insofar as He is the herald and founder of the Kingdom of God, and He bestows on us in seed His missionary and apostolic spirit. *Our task is to cooperate with the grace of the Sacrament by becoming ever more mature witnesses for Him to the world, even prepared to shed our blood if need be after His example and that of the Martyrs.*

Prayer for the Renewal of the Gift of Confirmation

HOLY Spirit, how solemn and full of heavenly blessing was the day on which I was signed with the chrism of salvation in the

Sacrament of Confirmation! You then took possession of my soul and made it Your temple and dwelling place. You came to help me grow in good and battle against all evil. You marked me indelibly as a soldier of Christ.

I thank You, Divine Spirit, for the fullness of graces and gifts that You bestowed on me in Your overflowing love. But when I reflect upon them, I am filled with shame and contrition at my slowness in responding to these graces and in keeping my solemn promise to be a faithful and steadfast Christian.

I have offended You and even driven You from my heart. Holy Spirit, I am heartily sorry for all the sins I have committed since the day of my Confirmation, because they have offended Your goodness and love.

I beg You, God Holy Spirit, remain with me constantly, and inflame my soul with Your eternal love. Never let me be separated from You by sin. I ask most humbly that I may be given strength to cooperate with Your graces at all times and never neglect the Commandments of God, the Precepts of the Church, or the duties of my calling. Let me rather die than ever grieve You by mortal sin.

I now renew the promise made at Confirmation, to live and die as a valiant soldier of Christ. God Holy Spirit, give me the grace to keep this resolution until death. Amen.

FIFTH DAY—THE SACRAMENT OF THE EUCHARIST

The Word of God

"Unless you eat the Flesh of the of the Son of Man and drink His Blood, you shall not have life in you." —Jn 6:54

Reflection

THE *Eucharist* unites us with Jesus and enables us to give glory to God and attain salvation for the world. It is a prayer of the whole Church in which we receive the Whole Christ: His Word, His Body, His Spirit. His Word tells us how we are to speak to God. His Body and Blood is the sole offering that is pleasing to the Father. And His Spirit is the One Who teaches us how to pray and what to pray for.

Thus, in the Eucharist, Christ assimilates us to Himself insofar as He is Love, and He gives us the spirit of His priesthood and victimhood. *Our task is to cooperate with the grace of the Sacrament by becoming even more united with Him, "the Person for others par excellence." We are to live in solidarity with and for others rather than for ourselves.*

Prayer To Receive All the Graces of Holy Communion

JESUS, I believe that Holy Communion unites my soul more closely with You. Even after Holy Communion You abide in me by Your grace and the action of the Holy Spirit.

The special effect of Holy Communion is to make me Christlike, not only by giving me sanctifying grace, but also by giving me actual graces to preserve Your Divine life in my soul. Through actual graces given during and after Holy Communion You help me to practice virtue and to become like You.

I beg You to abide in me through Holy Communion and the action of Your Holy Spirit. You want to be in me the source of all activity of my soul. Grant that my soul may remain given up to You and Your every wish, and that Your action may become so powerful that my soul may be carried on to ever greater holiness. Take possession of me and direct my whole life and reshape it according to Your great ideal. Live in me by grace and Your Holy Spirit. Through me may Your light shine, Your example radiate, Your life spread for the glory of God and the salvation of souls. Amen.

SIXTH DAY—THE SACRAMENT OF PENANCE

The Word of God

"Receive the Holy Spirit. Whose sins you shall forgive, they are forgiven them; and whose sins you shall retain, they are retained."   —Jn 20:23

Reflection

THROUGH the Sacrament of *Penance*, Jesus the Good Shepherd forgives our sins and sends His Holy Spirit once more to our soul to help us lead the Christian life and to grow spiritually. Penance not only forgives sins but also develops virtues in us that make us more Christlike.

Thus, in Penance, Christ assimilates us to Himself insofar as He is the victim of expiation for the sins of the world, and He gives us His spirit of penance. *Our task is to cooperate with the grace of the Sacrament by praying for those who do not pray and making reparation for those who do not make reparation.*

Prayer for the Grace of the Sacrament of Penance

MY DEAR God, I now renew the promises I have made in Baptism, and I give myself entirely to Your love and service. Give me the grace in the future to hate sin more than death itself and to avoid all such occasions and company as have in the past unhappily brought me to it.

Help me, O Lord, for I am weak. Strengthen my resolutions and give me sufficient grace to overcome the evil prompting of my nature. Never permit me to wound You again by sins. Refresh my soul that I may become strong in my determination to perform the duties of my state of life properly and fearlessly. Through Your Divine grace, without which I can do nothing, help me to live a good life, die a happy death, save my immortal soul, and be happy with You for all eternity in heaven. Amen.

SEVENTH DAY—THE SACRAMENT OF MATRIMONY

The Word of God

"For this cause, a man shall leave his father and mother and cleave to his wife; and the two shall become one flesh."   —Mt 19:5

Reflection

THE Sacrament of *Matrimony* gives us grace to enable spouses to fulfill their rights and duties to God, to each other, and to their children faithfully until death. The Holy Spirit breathes God's own love into the love between husband and wife so that as they selflessly share their life in God each becomes a minister of grace to the other.

Thus, in Matrimony, Christ assimilates us to Himself insofar as He is the Spouse of the Church, and He gives us His spirit of loving union. *The task of spouses is to cooperate with the grace of the Sacrament by loving one another as Christ loves the Church.*

Prayer for the Grace of Matrimony

O HOLY Spirit, Spirit of unity, Love, and Goodwill of Father and Son, You have made us one in the sacred union of marriage. Grant that, like the first Christians, we may be of one heart and one mind.

Make us respect one another, help one another in our striving for holiness, and support one another. Be our Guide, our Counselor, and our Consoler. Make us bear one another's burdens during our journey to heaven where we hope to live forever as adopted children of the Triune God. Amen.

EIGHTH DAY—THE SACRAMENT OF HOLY ORDERS

The Word of God

"As the Father has sent Me, I also send you." —Jn 20:21

Reflection

THE Sacrament of *Holy Orders* bestows a permanent charism or grace of the Holy Spirit enabling the recipients to guide and shepherd the faith community, proclaim and explain the Gospel, and guide and sanctify God's people.

Thus, in Holy Orders, Christ assimilates us to Himself insofar as He is the eternal High Priest, and He gives us the spirit of self-offering that He carried out in His Priesthood. *The task of those who have received Holy Orders is to cooperate with the grace of the Sacrament by utilizing their prophetic, liturgical, and pastoral function to show forth the love of the Father for the glory of God and the salvation of the world.*

Prayer for Those in Holy Orders

GOD Holy Spirit, Divine Fire, enkindle in all those who share the holy priesthood of Jesus Christ and Your apostolate the flames that transformed the disciples in the Upper

Room. They will then no longer be ordinary men, but men living to transfuse the Divine life into the souls of their fellow men.

Spirit of Light, imprint an indelible character of holiness on their souls, for their apostolate will be successful only in the measure in which they themselves live that supernatural life of which You are the sovereign Principle and Jesus Christ is the Source.

Holy Spirit of Wisdom, infuse Your grace into the hearts of the youth of our country. Call them in greater numbers to the holy priesthood and missionary life. Urge them on to be generous and to take upon themselves the work of God's Kingdom on earth.

Assured by the words of Jesus that what we ask in His Name will be granted, I entreat You in His Name to increase the number of vocations to the priesthood and religious state, and not to permit the work of the Church to be hampered for lack of worthy laborers. Amen.

NINTH DAY—THE SACRAMENT OF THE ANOINTING OF THE SICK

The Word of God

"Is anyone among you sick? Let him bring in the presbyters of the Church, and let them pray over him, anointing him with oil in the Name of the Lord."   —Jas 5:14

Reflection

THE *Anointing of the Sick* brings the whole person back to health, encourages trust in

God, and gives us strength to resist temptations and overcome anxiety about death. Besides forgiving the sins of the dying, it enables them to offer themselves, their lives, and their sufferings to God with sincere Christian resignation.

Thus in the Anointing of the Sick, Christ assimilates us to Himself insofar as He is the wonder worker and healer as well as the Man of Sorrows, and He gives us the spirit in which He accepted the Cross. *The task of those anointed is to cooperate with the grace of the Sacrament by transforming earthly trials into means of purification, tears into spiritual pearls, thorns into mystical roses, and ultimately death into eternal life.*

Prayer for the Grace of the Sacrament

O ALMIGHTY and merciful God, You have healed mankind by Your salvation and bestowed on it the gift of everlasting life; look graciously upon Your servants and comfort the souls that You have created. Free them from the stain of sin at the hour of death, so that they may be brought by Your Angels before You, their Maker.

Almighty God, have compassion on Your servants and through the power of this Sacrament strengthen us by Your grace. May the enemy not triumph over us in the hour of death, but rather may we be brought to everlasting life in the company of Your Angels. Amen.

NOVENA FOR THE FRUITS OF THE HOLY SPIRIT

MEDITATION

THE Holy Spirit guides us in the way of sanctification and salvation. As He descended upon Jesus at His Baptism by St. John, so the Spirit descends upon us at Baptism and inspires us to a loving union with God through actions and prayer.

Through the Church's Sacraments we have access to grace—the Divine Life of the Trinity. In its wake come the Gifts of the Holy Spirit, which help us to lead truly Christian lives by making us more alert to discern and more ready to carry out the Will of God.

In turn, the Gifts give rise to virtuous acts—good works, desires, and sentiments inspired in us by the Holy Spirit. In Galatians 5:22, St. Paul enumerates twelve such Fruits: Love, Joy, Peace, Patience, Longanimity, Goodness, Benignity, Mildness, Fidelity, Modesty, Continence, and Chastity.

46

All of these can be summed up in love of God and neighbor.

When the soul is docile to the inspirations of the Holy Spirit, it becomes a good tree that is known by its Fruits (see Mt 7:8-10).

(1) *Love (Charity)* means the Fruit found in those who are *wholly* committed and entirely delivered to the Holy Spirit's action. It consists in perfect love of God and neighbor.

(2) *Joy* means the *intense* and intimate satisfaction that persons experience when they realize they are in possession of their Sovereign Good. They realize they are infinitely loved by the God of Love and in turn they love God with the power of their free will.

(3) *Peace* is the quiet, *perfect* repose persons experience when they are wholly and perfectly submissive to the Divine Will.

(4) *Patience* means lovingly and fully accepting the trials that the Divine Goodness sees fit to let a person undergo.

(5) *Longanimity* consists in knowing how to wait, *feeling certain*, during trials, that God's moment will come, when He will fully aid the suffering person.

(6) *Goodness* here means truly desiring the good of all our brothers and sisters in Christ and also that of all our friends and our enemies, making no exception of any kind. This is the love of *perfect goodwill*.

(7) *Benignity* means to procure for your brothers and sisters in Christ, without any distinction of persons, *all the good* you are able to give them. It is the love of *beneficence*.

(8) *Mildness* means bearing with gentleness and patience all the defects of others, without ever yielding to improper anger. It is lovingly accepting—*always*—such troublesome things.

(9) *Fidelity* means *eagerly* rendering to all people everything you owe them. It is the *perfect* virtue of *justice.*

(10) *Modesty* means *always* and in every circumstance keeping the just and *golden mean,* the proper measure, and never falling into contrary excesses.

(11) *Continence* means *fully* controlling the disorderly movements of one's sensible nature, in particular the movements contrary to perfect chastity. This then is the *laborious* chastity of the soul that suffers such temptations.

(12) *Chastity* means perfect and *unalterable purity* when God, in His mercy, wants to preserve a person even from temptations against the virtue of *chastity.* Such, certainly, was the chastity of Jesus and Mary.

The Fruits embellish the Christian life and dispose souls to hear what God wills for us. They can be practiced even in the presence of great temptations if we flee the occasion and remain steadfast, knowing that God's grace will never be lacking.

The Word of God

"Every good tree bears good fruit, but the bad tree bears bad fruit. A good tree cannot bear bad fruit, nor can a bad tree bear good fruit. Therefore, by their fruits you will know them."   —Mt 7:17-20

"The fruit of the Spirit is: charity, joy, peace, patience, benignity, goodness, longanimity, mildness, faith, modesty, continence, chastity. Against such there is no law."

—Gal 5:22-23

"May you walk worthily of God and please Him in all things, bearing fruit in every good work and growing in knowledge of God."   —Col 1:10

NOVENA PRAYERS

Prayer for the Twelve Fruits of the Spirit

HOLY Spirit, eternal Love of the Father and the Son, kindly bestow on us the Fruit of *Charity*, that we may be united to You by Divine Love; the Fruit of *Joy*, that we may be filled with holy consolation; the Fruit of *Peace*, that we may enjoy tranquility of soul; and the Fruit of *Patience*, that we may endure humbly everything that may be opposed to our own desires.

Divine Spirit, be pleased to infuse in us the Fruit of *Longanimity*, that we may not be discouraged by delay but may persevere in prayer; the Fruit of *Goodness*, that we may be benevolent toward all; the Fruit of *Benignity*, that we may willingly relieve our neighbor's necessities; and the Fruit of *Kindness*, that we may subdue every rising of ill temper, stifle every murmur, and repress the susceptibilities of our nature in all our dealings with our neighbor.

Creator Spirit, graciously impart to us the Fruit of *Fidelity*, that we may rely with assured confidence on the Word of God; the Fruit of *Modesty*, that we may order our exterior regularly; and the Fruits of *Continence* and *Chastity*, that we may keep our bodies in such holiness as befits Your temple, so that having by Your assistance preserved our hearts pure on earth, we may merit in Jesus Christ, according to the words of the Gospel, to see God eternally in the glory of His Kingdom. Amen.

Litany of the Holy Spirit

(For Private Devotion)

LORD, have mercy.
Christ, have mercy.
Lord, have mercy.
Holy Spirit, hear us.
Holy Spirit, graciously hear us.
God, the Father of heaven, *have mercy on us.*
God, the Son, Redeemer of the world,*
God, the Holy Spirit,
Holy Trinity, one God,
Holy Spirit, Who proceed from the Father,
Holy Spirit, coequal with the Father and the Son,
Promise of the Father, most bounteous,
Gift of God most high,
Ray of heavenly Light,
Author of all good,
Source of living Water,
Consuming Fire,
Burning Love,
Spiritual Unction,
Spirit of truth and power,
Spirit of wisdom and understanding,
Spirit of counsel and fortitude,
Spirit of knowledge and piety,
Spirit of fear of the Lord,
Spirit of compunction,
Spirit of grace and prayer,
Spirit of charity, peace, and joy,
Spirit of patience,
Spirit of longanimity and goodness,
Spirit of benignity and mildness,
Spirit of fidelity,
Spirit of modesty and continence,
Spirit of chastity,
Spirit of adoption of sons of God,
Holy Spirit, comforter,
Holy Spirit, sanctifier,
You Who in the beginning moved upon the waters,
You through Whom spoke holy men of God,
You Who overshadowed Mary,
You by Whom Mary conceived Christ,
You Who descend upon men at Baptism,
You Who, on the Day of Pentecost, appeared through fiery tongues,
You by Whom we are reborn,
You Who dwell in us as in a temple,
You Who govern and animate the Church,
You Who fill the whole world,
That You may renew the face of the earth,
we beseech You, hear us.

Have mercy on us is repeated after each invocation.

That You may shed your Light upon us,**

That You may pour your Love into our hearts,

That You may inspire us to love our neighbor,

That You may teach us to ask for the graces we need,

That You may enlighten us with Your heavenly inspirations,

That You may guide us in the way of holiness,

That You may make us obedient to Your commandments,

That You may teach us how to pray,

That You may always pray with us,

That You may inspire us with horror for sin,

That You may direct us in the practice of virtue,

That You may make us persevere in a holy life,

That You may make us faithful to our vocation,

That You may grant us good priests and bishops,

That You may give us good Christian families,

That you may grant us a spiritual renewal of the Church,

That that you may guide and console the Holy Father,

Lamb of God, You take away the sins of the world; *spare us, O Lord.*

Lamb of God, You take away the sins of the world, *graciously hear us, O Lord.*

Lamb of God, You take away the sins of the world; *have mercy on us.*

Holy Spirit, hear us.

Holy Spirit, graciously hear us.

Lord, have mercy.

Christ, have mercy.

Lord, have mercy.

℣. Create a clean heart in us.

℟. Renew a right spirit in us.

**We beseech You, hear us* is repeated after each invocation.

LET us pray. Merciful Father, grant that Your Divine Spirit may cleanse, inflame, and enlighten our minds and hearts. Enable us to be fruitful in good works for the glory of Your Majesty and the spiritual and material well-being of all people. We ask this through Jesus Christ Your Son and the Holy Spirit. ℟. *Amen.*

NOVENA TO THE HOLY SPIRIT IN THE LIGHT OF VATICAN II

MEDITATION

THE Second Vatican Council was aptly described by the Extraordinary Synod of 1985 as "a grace of God and a gift of the Holy Spirit." Indeed, when convoked by Pope John XXIII, it was immediately placed under the aegis of the Holy Spirit in the prayer the Pope composed to be offered in preparation for the Council. This is completely in accord with the teaching of the Church that Ecumenical Councils are inspired by the Holy Spirit especially when making dogmatic statements. A Council is, in effect, an epiphany of the Holy Spirit.

In Vatican II, the influence of the Spirit is seen most powerfully in the *Dogmatic Constitution on the Church* and the *Dogmatic Constitution on Sa-*

cred *Scripture* as well as in parts of the decrees that recall explicit Catholic dogmas, particularly the *Constitution on the Church in the Modern World.*

The Council also affirmed: "Christ is now at work in the hearts of men and women through the energy of His Spirit. He not only arouses a desire for the age to come but also vivifies, purifies, and strengthens those generous impulses by which the human family strives to render its life more human and to submit the whole earth to this goal" *(Constitution on the Church in the Modern World,* no. 38).

At the same time, the Council also issued some magnificent texts concerning the Holy Spirit. By making a Novena in the light of Vatican II, we can meditate on these texts and pray in that same vein. In this way, we cannot but get to know the Holy Spirit better, be moved to have frequent recourse to Him, and render glory to the Triune God.

FIRST DAY—THE SPIRIT AND THE CHURCH

Teaching of Vatican II

"Christ sent from the Father His Holy Spirit, Who was to carry on inwardly His saving work and prompt the Church to spread out. Doubtless, the Holy Spirit was already at work in the world before Christ was glorified. Yet on the day of Pentecost, He came down upon the disciples to remain with them forever" (see Jn 14:16).
  —*Decree on the Missionary Activity of the Church,* no. 4

"The Holy Spirit was sent that He might continually sanctify the Church, and thus, all those who believe would have access through Christ in one Spirit to the Father. He is the Spirit of Life, a fountain of water springing up to life eternal. To humans dead in sin, the Father gives life through Him, until, in Christ, He brings to life their mortal bodies."　　　　*—Constitution on the Church,* no. 4

"The Spirit dwells in the Church and in the hearts of the faithful, as in a temple. In them He prays on their behalf and bears witness to the fact that they are adopted children.

"The Church, which the Spirit guides in the way of all truth and which He unified in communion and in works of ministry, He both equips and directs with hierarchical and charismatic gifts and adorns with His fruits.

"By the power of the Gospel He makes the Church keep the freshness of youth. Uninterruptedly He renews her and leads her to perfect union with her Spouse. The Spirit and the Bride both say to Jesus, the Lord, 'Come!' "
　　　　—Constitution on the Church, no. 4

Prayer for the Church

IN UNION with the Praying Church we pray: Send forth Your Spirit and renew the world.

O God, in the beginning You created heaven and earth, and in the fullness of time You restored all things through Christ. Renew the world now through Your Holy Spirit.

You formed man and blew into him the Breath of life. Send now Your Spirit into the Church that she may give new life to mankind.

Enlighten all human beings by the Light of the Spirit and dispel the darkness of our time. Change hatred into love, sorrow into joy, warfare into peace.

You introduce human beings into life and glory, through the Holy Spirit. Grant to the deceased the joys of love in the Heavenly Kingdom.

You promised the Holy Spirit, that He might teach us all things and remind us of all that Your Son Jesus Christ has deigned to teach. Send us Your Spirit to strengthen our Faith, our Hope, and our Love.

This we ask, Heavenly Father, through Jesus Christ, Your Son Who lives with You in the unity of the Holy Spirit. Amen.

SECOND DAY—THE SPIRIT, SCRIPTURE, AND TRADITION

Teaching of Vatican II

"Sacred Scripture is the Word of God inasmuch as it is consigned to writing *under the inspiration of the Divine Spirit. Sacred Tradition* takes the Word of God entrusted by Christ the Lord and the *Holy Spirit to the Apostles,* and hands it on to their successors in its full purity, so that led by the light of the Spirit of truth, they may in proclaiming it preserve this Word of God faithfully, explain it, and make it more widely known.

"Consequently it is not from Sacred Scripture alone that the Church draws her certainty about everything that has been revealed. Therefore both Sacred Tradition and Sacred Scripture are to be accepted and venerated with the same sense of loyalty and reverence."

—*Constitution on Divine Revelation,* no. 9

Prayer Before Reading the Bible

O KING of glory, Lord of Hosts, You triumphantly ascended the heavens. Leave us not as orphans but send us the Promised of the Father, the Spirit of Truth.

We implore You, O Lord, that the Counselor Who proceeds from You may enlighten our souls and infuse into them all truth, as Your Son has promised. O God, Father of our Lord Jesus Christ, be pleased to grant us, according to the riches of Your glory, that Christ by faith may dwell in our hearts, which, rooted and grounded in charity, may acknowledge the love of Christ, surpassing all knowledge. We ask this through Christ our Lord. Amen.

THIRD DAY—FREEDOM CONFERRED BY THE SPIRIT

Teaching of Vatican II

"The gifts of the Spirit are diverse: while He calls some to give clear witness to the desire for a heavenly home and to keep that desire green among the human family, He summons others to dedicate themselves to the earthly service of human beings and to make ready the material of the celestial realm by this ministry of theirs.

"Yet [the Spirit] *frees all of them* so that by putting aside love of self and bringing all earthly resources into the service of human life they can devote themselves to that future when humanity itself will become an offering accepted by God." —*Constitution on the Church in the Modern World,* no. 38

Prayer To Know One's Vocation

O LORD, I beg You to send down the Holy Spirit upon me to enlighten me. May I know the designs of Your Providence concerning me and, filled with a sincere desire for my soul's salvation, say with the rich young man of the Gospel, "What must I do to be saved?" All states of life are before me; but, still undecided as to what to do, I await Your commands.

I offer myself to You without restriction, without reserve, with a most perfect submission.

Far be it from me, O Lord, to oppose Your wisdom and, unfaithful to the inspiration of Your grace, to strive to subject the Will of the Creator to the caprice of the creature. It is not for the servant to choose the way in which he will serve the Master. May You command for me what You please. My lot is in Your hands. "Speak, Lord, for Your servant is listening."

O Spirit of Piety, inspire the affections of my parents and guide their projects according to Your wisdom. O Holy Spirit, I sincerely desire to consult You Who are all-wise. Grant that my parents also may submit themselves to Your decrees, faithfully and without reserve. Amen.

FOURTH DAY—THE SPIRIT AND FAITH

Teaching of Vatican II

"To make [a free] act of faith, the grace of God and the *interior help of the Holy Spirit* must precede and assist, moving the heart and turning it to God, opening the eyes of the mind and giving joy and ease to everyone in assenting to the truth and believing it.

"To bring about an ever deeper understanding of Revelation the same Holy Spirit constantly brings faith to completion by His Gifts."

—*Constitution on Divine Revelation*, no. 5

Prayer of Thanksgiving for the Gift of Faith

O GOD the Holy Spirit, in Whom I have been baptized in the unity of that Body of which Christ is the Head, make me a partaker of all those graces that flow from the Divine Head upon all the members of His Mystical Body. Preserve me in the unity of faith and the bond of peace.

I thank You, O Adorable Spirit, for the signal grace of having been born in the pale of the true Church. I beg of You to make this union of mine with the Church ever more close, more intimate, more prolific in grace and sanctification. Make me not only one body but also one mind with the holy Church, the pillar and ground of truth. Amen.

FIFTH DAY—THE SPIRIT AND THE LAITY

Teaching of Vatican II

"For the exercise of the [Christian] apostolate, the Holy Spirit *Who sanctifies the People of God* through ministry and the Sacraments *gives the faithful special Gifts also* (see 1 Cor 12:7), allotting them to everyone according as He wills (1 Cor 12:11) in order that individuals, administering grace to others just as they have received it, may also be 'good stewards of the manifold grace of God' (1 Pt 4:10), to build up the whole body in charity (see Eph 4:16).

"From the acceptance of these charismas, including those which are more elementary, there arise for each believer the right and duty to use them in the Church and in the world for the good of and the building up of the Church, in the freedom of the Holy Spirit 'Who breathes where He wills (Jn 3:8).' . . .

"Lay persons should learn especially how to perform the mission of Christ and the Church by basing their lives on belief in the Divine Mystery of Creation and Redemption and by *being sensitive to the movement of the Holy Spirit* Who gives life to the People of God and Who urges all to love God the Father as well as the world and others in Him."

—*Decree on the Apostolate of the Laity,* no. 3

Prayer for the Laity

O HOLY Spirit, Eternal Love of the Father and the Son, take me to Yourself as Your child of predilection. Direct me constantly and uphold me in the path of virtue. Illumine my mind, sanctify my soul, and take possession of my entire being. Help me to exercise my lay apostolate where I work or practice my profession, or study or reside, or spend any leisure time, or have my companionships.

Grant that I may become the light of the world by conforming my life to my faith. By practicing honesty in all my dealings, may I attract all whom I meet to the love of the true and the good, and ultimately to the Church and to Christ.

Inspire me to share in the living conditions as well as the labors, sorrows, and aspirations of my brothers and sisters, thus preparing their hearts for the worship of Your saving grace. Enable me to perform my domestic, social, and professional duties with such Christian generosity that my way of acting will penetrate the world of life and labor.

Teach me to cooperate with all men and women of goodwill in promoting whatever is true, whatever is holy, whatever is lovable. Let me complement the testimony of my life with the testimony of the word, so that I will proclaim Christ to those brothers and sisters who can hear the Gospel through no one else but me. Amen.

SIXTH DAY—THE SPIRIT AND MARRIED PEOPLE

Teaching of Vatican II

"Christian spouses have a special Sacrament by which they are fortified and receive a kind of consecration in the duties and dignity of their state. By virtue of this Sacrament, as spouses fulfill their conjugal and family obligation, they are penetrated with the Spirit of Christ, Who suffuses their whole lives with faith, hope, and charity.

"Thus they increasingly advance the perfection of their own personalities, as well as their mutual sanctification, and hence contribute jointly to the glory of God."

—*Constitution on the Church in the Modern World,*
no. 48

Prayer to the Spirit for Our Home

O ETERNAL Spirit of Love, Dove of Peace, and Bond of Unity in the Blessed Trinity, preserve love, unity, and peace in our home. Make of it a faithful reproduction of the holy house of Nazareth, which was so pleasing to You. Bind us all together, not merely by carnal ties but also by the golden bonds of charity, prayer, and mutual service. Make us one heart and one soul.

By the Gift of Piety, help us to forgive and forget the little grievances that the vicissitudes of life and diversity of character may foster among us. Wherever duty may call us, let us never bring dishonor upon our home and our family. Ward off from our home the spirit of pride, irreligion, and worldliness. Do not allow the lax principles and perverse maxims of the world to take root among us.

Teach us to love and respect that Christian modesty which reigned supreme in the holy house of Nazareth. As by Your help we live in unity here below, give us, we beg You, the grace of final perseverance, so that together we may praise You and love You through a happy eternity. Amen.

SEVENTH DAY—THE SPIRIT AND THE RELIGIOUS LIFE

Teaching of Vatican II

"The adaptation and renewal of the religious life includes both the constant return to the sources of all Christian life and to the original spirit of the institutes and their adaptation to the changed conditions of our time. This renewal must be advanced under the inspiration of the Holy Spirit and the guidance of the Church."

—*Decree on the Adaptation and Renewal of Religious Life,* no. 2

Prayer for Religious

O HOLY Spirit, Eternal Love of the Father and the Son, guide Your people in the way of salvation and watch over those who have left all things to give themselves entirely to You. By following Christ and renouncing worldly power and profit, may they serve God and their brothers and sisters faithfully in the spirit of poverty and humility. Amen.

EIGHTH DAY—THE SPIRIT AND THE PRIESTLY LIFE
Teaching of Vatican II

"In order that, in all conditions of life, priests may be able to grow in union with Christ, they possess the exercise of their conscious ministry. They also enjoy the common and particular means, old and new, which the Spirit never ceases to arouse in the People of God and which the Church commends, and sometimes commands, for the sanctification of her members. . . .

"Nourished by spiritual reading, under the light of faith, they can more diligently seek signs of God's Will and impulses of His grace in the various events of life, and so from day to day become more docile to the mission they have assumed in the Holy Spirit."

—*Decree on the Ministry and Life of Priests,* no. 18

"Holiness does much for priests in carrying on a fruitful ministry. Although Divine grace could use unworthy ministers to effect the work of salvation, yet for the most part God chooses, to show forth His wonders, those who are more open to the power and direction of the Holy Spirit, and who can by reason of their close union with Christ and their holiness of life say with St. Paul: 'And yet I am alive; or rather, not I; it is Christ that lives in me' (Gal 2:20)."

—*Decree on the Ministry and Life of Priests,* no. 12

Prayer for Priests

O Holy Spirit, Jesus has ordained that the Word should be preached and the Sacraments administered by the ministry of priests. Grant them, we beg You, Your continual Divine assistance.

Let them remember that in performing their tasks they are never alone. Relying on Your ever present assistance and believing in Christ Who called them to share in His priesthood, may they devote themselves to their ministry with complete trust, knowing that You can intensify in them the ability to love.

Let them also be mindful that they have as partners their brothers in the priesthood and indeed the faithful of the entire world. For they cooperate in carrying out the saving plan of Christ, which is brought to fulfillment only in degrees through the collaboration of many ministries in the building up of Christ's Body until the full measure of His Manhood is achieved. Amen.

NINTH DAY—THE SPIRIT AND HOLINESS

Teaching of Vatican II

"It is not only through the Sacraments and the ministries of the Church that the Holy Spirit sanctifies and leads the People of God and enriches it with virtues, but allotting His Gifts to everyone according as He wills, He distributes special graces among the faithful of every rank. By these Gifts He makes them fit and ready to undertake the various tasks and offices that contribute toward the renewal and building up of the Church. . . .

"These charisms, whether they be the more outstanding or the more simple and widely diffused, are to be received with thanksgiving and consolation for they are perfectly suited to and useful for the needs of the Church." *—Constitution on the Church, no. 12*

Prayer to the Spirit for Holiness

DIVINE Spirit, all of us children of God are an edifice built on the foundation of the Apostles and Prophets with Jesus Christ as the chief cornerstone. In Christ the whole structure is being closely fitted together by You to become God's temple consecrated in the Lord.

St. Paul warns me: "Do not extinguish the Spirit." Never let me despise the utterances You inspire, but accept them all.

Give me the grace to hold on to that which is good, and have nothing to do with any kind of evil.

Divine Author of grace, make me perfect in holiness. May every part of my being, soul and body, be preserved blameless for the day when our Lord Jesus Christ shall come.

You have called me to holiness. Make me worthy of that call. By Your power accomplish all my yearning for moral goodness, and bring to perfection the actions my faith prompts.

In this way may the Name of our Lord Jesus be glorified in me, and may I be glorified in Him by Your grace, which He merited for me.

God's love is poured forth in our hearts by You, Holy Spirit, Who have been given us. Pour forth that grace into my own heart in rich abundance. Amen.